# F~4 PHANTOM II

## Series Editor : Christopher Chant

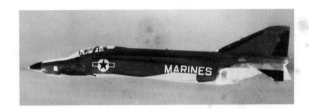

Foulis

Haynes

Titles in the *Super Profile* series:

*Boeing 707*

*B-29 Superfortress*

*Harrier*

*Sea King*

*Super Etendard*

*F-4 Phantom II*

**ISBN 0 85429 376 0**

**A FOULIS Aircraft Book**

Further titles in this series will be published at regular intervals. For information on new titles please contact your bookseller or write to the publisher

First published 1983

© **1983 Winchmore Publishing Services Limited**

*Published by:*
**Haynes Publishing Group**
Sparkford,
Yeovil,
Somerset BA22 7JJ

*Distributed in North America by:*
**Haynes Publications Inc.**
861 Lawrence Drive,
Newbury Park,
California 91320, USA

*Produced by:*
**Winchmore Publishing Services Limited,**
40 Triton Square,
London, NW1 3HG

Picture research Jonathan Moore
Printed in Hong Kong by
Lee Fung Asco Limited.

# Contents

# Genesis

The first McDonnell Phantom, the US Navy's FH-1, had its maiden flight in prototype form in January 1945, and entered service some two years later as the world's first carrier-based jet fighter. During the next few years the company provided the navy with a succession of new fighters of increasing power. The F2H Banshee, flown in January 1947 and in service just over two years later, used two 3,000-lb (1,361-kg) st (static thrust) Westinghouse J34 engines in place of its predecessor's 1,600-lb (726-kg) st J30s; and the F3H Demon, flown in August 1951 and in service from March 1953, had a single 7,200-lb (3,266-kg) st Westinghouse J40.

Only 60 of the original Phantom were built, but production of the Banshee and Demon reached totals of 895 and 517 respectively. However, by the time the Demons were entering US Navy service, the McDonnell Aircraft Company was already at work on a new design that was to eclipse the achievements of the earlier models completely. The new fighter, also named Phantom, would remain in production for a good 20 years, and the total of 5,288 built would serve not only with the US Navy, Air Force and Marine Corps, but also with the air forces of another ten countries as well as the Royal Navy.

The reasons for the new fighter's unparalleled success can be expressed in a number of ways. In terms of performance it flew faster and higher than any other fighter of its generation, climbed more quickly and stayed airborne longer. Operationally it delivered more ordnance, whether air-to-air or air-to-ground, more accurately, and had greater versatility. It was safer and better-equipped than any rival.

In fact, the only department in which the Phantom II failed to excel was that of aesthetics. With its drooping nose, deep fuselage, long tail, up-tilted wings and down-canted tailplane, the new McDonnell fighter provoked plenty of adverse comments on its appearance. Pilots also found cause for complaint: when the US Air Force decided to follow the Navy and buy its own Phantoms, adding controls and instrumentation for air-to-surface weapons, the cockpit layout became extremely cluttered; over Vietnam the hydraulic flight control systems proved vulnerable to ground fire, the smoky engines proved something of a liability, and there was a blind area looking aft from the cockpit.

But when an aircraft designed as a fleet-defence fighter, constrained by the need to fit into 56-ft (17-m) deck elevators, and intended to use radar-guided missiles to destroy attackers, turns out to be one of the best close-support, long-range bomber, reconnaissance and defence suppression aircraft around, such criticisms begin to seem irrelevant. Having set a new standard in fighter design, the Phantom went on to do most other jobs better than purpose-built competitors. And, perhaps most remarkable of all, in an era of unprecedented technological progress, it took fifteen years for anyone to build a better fighter.

The first of two XF4H-1 prototypes of the Phantom during an early test flight in 1958. No radar is fitted, and the Sparrow missiles under the fuselage are dummies.

# Design and Development

The name Phantom II was first conferred on a design designated FH3-G. This was completed in mock-up form in 1954, after McDonnell's proposal for a supersonic carrier-based fighter had been rejected in favour of the Chance Vought F-8 Crusader, and represented the fruits of the company's extensive research into future US Navy requirements. With a broad, high-lift wing, twin Wright J65 Sapphire engines, four 20-mm cannon in the nose and a total of 11 stores pylons, the new design combined features of the later fighter-bomber versions of the Demon with a predicted performance at least matching that of the supersonic F-101 Voodoo currently being built as a long-range escort and penetration fighter for the USAF.

By October 1954 the Bureau of Aeronautics had signified its intention to buy two examples of the F3H-G under the attack designation YAH-1. These were regarded as essentially experimental aircraft, hence the Y for evaluation. A change of powerplant to the new J79 engine then being developed by the General Electric company was specified, but the requirement was in other respects vague. The choice of powerplant was to prove significant. Development of the J79 began in 1952, and it represented the first American turbojet designed to use variable stators for higher compression.

In its basic form a turbojet engine compresses air drawn in at the front, adds fuel in a combustion chamber, and passes part of the hot gas resulting from combustion through a turbine which drives the compressor, while the rest is expelled as a hot, fast-moving gas jet to provide thrust. In a centrifugal-flow turbojet, the compressor operates as a simple centrifugal fan, but the addition of fixed stator blades between the rows of rotating blades in axial-flow engines enables the frontal area to be reduced.

Increased pressure ratios can be obtained by bleeding off some of the air from the front of the compressor, to avoid too much air choking the final stages, or by using separate low-pressure and high-pressure spools of blades, each driven by its own turbine. The third method, used in the J79, makes the stator blades adjustable in incidence to match the rate of flow required. The first six of the J79's 17 rows of stator blades were made variable in incidence, resulting in an extremely powerful and efficient engine, weighing nearly a third less than contemporary engines of equivalent power. With the addition of afterburning — the combustion of further fuel in the exhaust stream — and a variable nozzle, it became the first production engine capable of operating at Mach 2.

In April 1955 a definite requirement was presented to McDonnell. Instead of the AH-1, the Navy had decided on a long-range, high-altitude interceptor for fleet defence. The guns were deleted in favour of a guided missile armament and the new fighter was to be equipped for all-weather operation, which meant the addition of a second crew member. By July the designation had been changed to F4H-1, following the approval of preliminary design studies, and the two prototypes already ordered were to be supplemented by five pre-production examples.

With the J79 already approaching its first flight test by this stage, the aircraft was redesigned to take full advantage of the promised power. The inner faces of the air intakes were mounted on either side of the fuselage, with a gap to keep them clear of the slow-moving boundary layer air, and the deep narrow ducts were provided with adjustable inlets. Boundary layer air was filtered out inside the ducts, and big doors in the bottoms could be opened by rams for full-power operation at low speed, such as during the take-off run. The intended powerplant, the 10,900-lb (4,944-kg) J79-8, was not available in time, and the first prototype XF4H-1 was powered by 9,300-lb (4,218-kg) J79-3As provided by the USAF. Thereafter 10,350-lb (4,695-kg) J79-2s or -2As were used, resulting in the designation F4H-1F being applied to initial production models, the F suffix indicating a non-standard powerplant under the US Navy system in force at the time.

The high power and increased maximum speed of Mach 2 specified for the new interception role led to further design changes. Wind tunnel tests revealed a severe lack of stability at the proposed higher speed, resulting in the adoption of another of the Phantom's characteristic features. This involved the outer wing panels being given increased chord, along with 12° dihedral, to produce the dog-tooth leading edge. This eliminated the instability, and reduced the wing-tip stalling speed, which had been found to be another problem with the original wing swept at a conventional 45°. At the same time, the one-piece tailplane, which combined the functions of stabiliser and elevator, was canted down at an angle of 23° to keep it clear of downwash from the wings at high angles of attack, and to cancel out the tendency to roll in yawing flight imparted by the outer wing dihedral.

Other changes were dictated

## Structure

1 Side-folding radome
2 Front pressure bulkhead
3 Martin-Baker MK5 seats
4 Rear pressure bulkhead
5 Canopy pneumatic jack
6 Retracting steps
7 Chem-milled duct walls
8 Windscreen/canopy frames (stretch-formed extrusions)
9 Top longeron
10 Fabricated main frame
11 Machined main frame
12 Titanium formers
13 Titanium skin and frames
14 Glass-fibre tip
15 Machine milled cap strip
16 Chem-milled skin
17 Bonded honeycomb
18 Forged light-alloy frames
19 Titanium inner skin
20 Stainless-steel shingled blast panels
21 Drag-chute stowage and door
22 Titanium spars
23 Stainless-steel rib
24 Light alloy rib
25 Steel hinge fitting
26 Stainless-steel mass-balancer
27 Titanium skin
28 Light alloy skin
29 Catapult strop fitting
30 Multi-bolt wing/fuselage fixing
31 Machined light alloy spar
32 Forged ribs
33 Taper-machined torque-box skin panels
34 Top to bottom skin ties
35 Inter-skin web
36 Bonded honeycomb skin
37 Alclad ribs
38 Extruded stringers
39 Taper chem-milled access door
40 Pylon mount
41 Fold jack
42 Latch pins
43 Latch pin actuator

## A—Air systems

A 1 Equipment refrigeration unit (cockpit unit stbd side)
A 2 Ram-air intake
A 3 Heat exchanger
A 4 Radar cooling air
A 5 Engine bleed-air
A 6 Radar liquid-air heat-exchanger
A 7 Liquid-air coolant pump
A 8 Demisting air
A 9 Rain clearance air
A10 Engine bleed to leading edge BLC duct
A11 Engine bleed to flap blowing duct
A12 BLC slots
A13 Tail cone cooling-air intake
A14 Fuel-tank cooling air between skins
A15 Lox container (evaporator behind seat)

## P—Power plant

P 1 Fixed splitter plate (ramp)
P 2 Variable ramp
P 3 Hinge line
P 4 Boundary layer bleed perforations
P 5 Boundary layer bleed out
P 6 Rotary action spill valve
P 7 Rolls-Royce RB.168-25R engine
P 8 Oil tank
P 9 De-icing air
P10 Cooling air out
P11 Auxiliary-air door (also under fuselage)
P12 Igniter box
P13 Access doors (full length of engine bay)
P14 Variable ejector nozzle
P15 Nozzle actuators
P16 Air seal
P17 Forward mount link (thrust lug inboard)
P18 Aft mounting ring

## E—Emergency equipment and ground supply

E1 Auxiliary ram-air turbine
E2 Actuator
E3 Main-gear lowering air bottles
E4 Brake air bottle
E5 Nose-gear lowering air bottle
E6 Flap air bottle
E7 External power supply receptacle
E8 Hydraulic power control and external power connect

## C—Control system

C 1 Throttles
C 2 Flap
C 3 Emergency ram-air turbine
C 4 Motional pick-up transducer on control column
C 5 Aileron linkage
C 6 Lateral auto-pilot servo
C 7 Aileron droop actuator
C 8 Aileron power unit
C 9 Aileron damper
C10 Drooping ailerons (30° down 1° up)
C11 Aileron hinge (lower surface)
C12 Flutter damping hinge unit
C13 Airbrake (45° down)
C14 Airbrake jack
C15 Spoilers (max up 45°)
C16 Spoiler jack
C17 Blown plain flap
C18 Flap jack
C19 Leading edge flap
C20 Hinge
C21 Actuator
C22 Tailplane linkage
C23 Tailplane cables
C24 Tailplane power-unit
C25 Tailplane feel system
C26 Feel system ram-air
C27 Fixed inverted slat
C28 Rudder feel system
C29 Rudder power unit
C30 Mass balance
C31 Hook
C32 Hook actuator

## U—Undercarriage

U1 Steering power unit
U2 Gear door
U3 40 in catapult extension
U4 Main gear jack
U5 Shorten on retraction' link
U6 Up lock
U7 Tie down

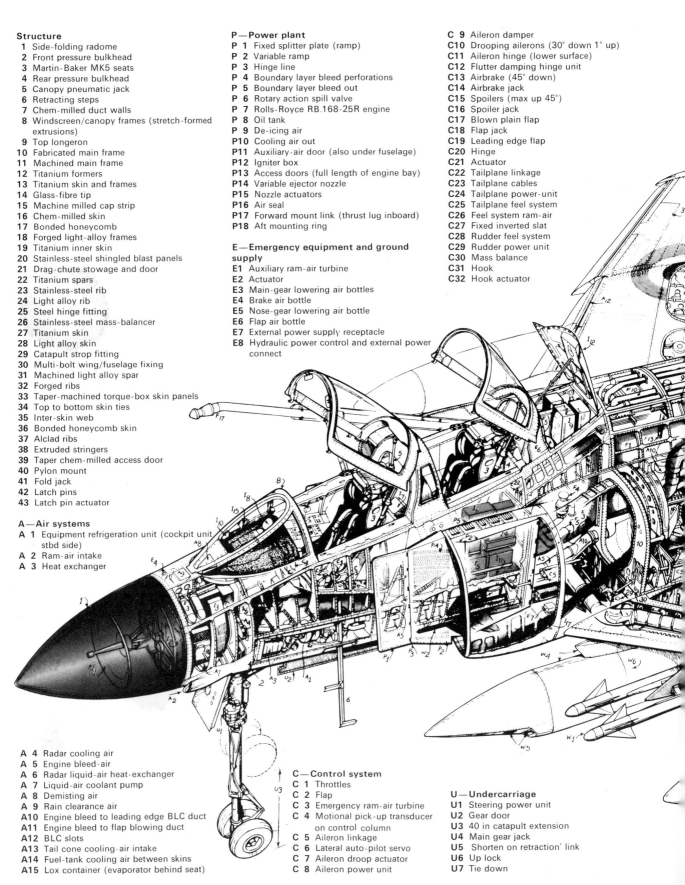

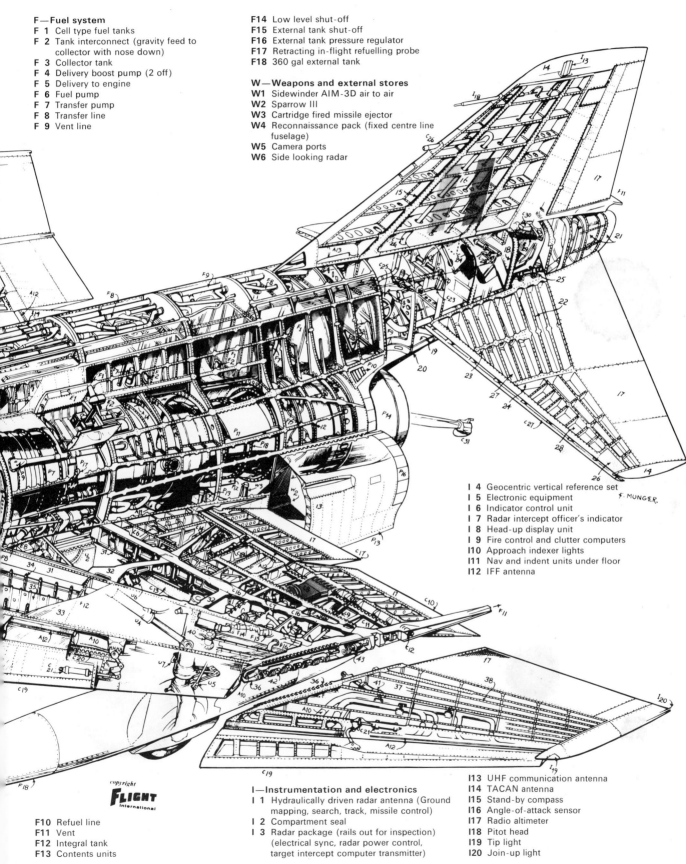

**F—Fuel system**
F 1  Cell type fuel tanks
F 2  Tank interconnect (gravity feed to collector with nose down)
F 3  Collector tank
F 4  Delivery boost pump (2 off)
F 5  Delivery to engine
F 6  Fuel pump
F 7  Transfer pump
F 8  Transfer line
F 9  Vent line

F14  Low level shut-off
F15  External tank shut-off
F16  External tank pressure regulator
F17  Retracting in-flight refuelling probe
F18  360 gal external tank

**W—Weapons and external stores**
W1  Sidewinder AIM-3D air to air
W2  Sparrow III
W3  Cartridge fired missile ejector
W4  Reconnaissance pack (fixed centre line fuselage)
W5  Camera ports
W6  Side looking radar

I 4  Geocentric vertical reference set
I 5  Electronic equipment
I 6  Indicator control unit
I 7  Radar intercept officer's indicator
I 8  Head-up display unit
I 9  Fire control and clutter computers
I10  Approach indexer lights
I11  Nav and indent units under floor
I12  IFF antenna

F. MUNGER.

F10  Refuel line
F11  Vent
F12  Integral tank
F13  Contents units

**I—Instrumentation and electronics**
I 1  Hydraulically driven radar antenna (Ground mapping, search, track, missile control)
I 2  Compartment seal
I 3  Radar package (rails out for inspection) (electrical sync, radar power control, target intercept computer transmitter)

I13  UHF communication antenna
I14  TACAN antenna
I15  Stand-by compass
I16  Angle-of-attack sensor
I17  Radio altimeter
I18  Pitot head
I19  Tip light
I20  Join-up light

by the revised armament. The missile selected was the Raytheon AIM-7C Sparrow, a semi-active radar homing development of the beam-riding AIM-7A, first used to arm the F3H Demon in 1955. The missiles themselves were mounted in recesses underneath the fuselage, and launched by explosive charges ejecting them downwards just before the motor ignited. The missile guidance radar was the APA-157, produced by Westinghouse, which illuminated the target with a continuous-wave signal, allowing the missiles to home on the reflected signal. A second cockpit was provided for the radar systems operator, both men having Martin-Baker ejection

seats and individual canopies opening to the rear.

The basic design was finalised in August 1956, and construction of the first prototype was begun in the same month. By the end of the year a further 16 pre-production F4H-1s had been ordered, and the first prototype was completed in April 1958, making its first flight with the J79-3As the following month. Flight testing of the prototype and pre-production aircraft was accompanied by progressive improvement of the Phantom's capabilities. The replacement of the J79-3A with the more powerful -2A engines gave an increase in afterburning thrust from 14,800 lb (6,713 kg) to 16,150 lb (7,326 kg), and this

powerplant was used on all 23 of the initial F4H-1s.

The mission requirements for the F4H included the ability to take off from a carrier deck, fly out to a position 250 miles (400 km) away, and maintain a combat air patrol for up to two hours before returning. Accordingly, the internal and wing fuel tanks were supplemented by the provision of attachment points on

*Right* and *below right:* The rear cockpit of an F-4E.
*Below:* The tail end of a Phantom showing the pivot seat for the one-piece stabilator, the vent pipe to the fuselage fuel tanks and the hinged tail cone which covers the drag chute housing.

the fuselage centreline for a 500-gallon (600-US gallon/2,270-litre) external tank. In addition, a folding flight refuelling probe was fitted on the right side of the forward fuselage. This had a capacity of 1,700 lb/min (770 kg/min) and could be used either for conventional probe-and-drogue refuelling, or for 'buddy' refuelling from another Phantom. By 1960 the latter technique was being practised with the aircraft flying at supersonic speeds.

Flight controls were also improved. On the seventh Phantom a system of boundary-layer control was introduced, using hot air bled from the engine compressor. This was blown along the droop flaps on the wing leading edges and along the wings ahead of the trailing edge flaps. Another innovation on this example was the installation of an infra-red seeker in a bullet fairing under the nose to detect the heat radiated by the engine exhaust of hostile aircraft. The seeker, designated AAA-4, could be used either independently to search for a target, or to lock on to a target

designated by the radar system. It could then designate the target to the heat-seeking head of an infra-red homing missile. In order to utilise this capacity a pylon was added under each wing to carry either a Sparrow or two AIM-9 (originally AAM-N-7) Sidewinder missiles, the original version of which entered service in 1956. The eleventh example was also fitted with a total of six wing and two fuselage pylons, with which it demonstrated an ability to carry 22 500-lb (227-kg) bombs.

Meanwhile, the radar system was also being developed. By the time the nineteenth Phantom was completed, the dish antenna for the radar had grown to a diameter of 32 in (81 cm) for the Westinghouse APQ-72 radar, which replaced the earlier APQ-50 with 24-in (61-cm) dish. The same antenna was used to transmit the guidance signal for the Sparrows. The result was the large pointed radome, designed to be swung open for access to the equipment inside, which gave the Phantom its characteristic droop-nosed

Part of the final assembly line in October 1963, when production of the USAF's F-4C was getting under way alongside that of the F-4B for the US Navy and Marine Corps.

appearance. Principal functions of the APQ-72 were acquisition and tracking of airborne targets.

At the same time as the new radar was installed, the original flush canopy was made slightly higher to accommodate the raising of the seats for improved visibility. This F4H-1, with the bigger radome, new canopy and stores pylons, was the first to achieve the basic configuration of subsequent production models. In the meantime, following competitive trials with the Chance Vought F8U-3 Crusader III, the Phantom had been confirmed as the new US Navy interceptor and a further 24 F4H-1s were ordered in December 1958, bringing the total number to 47. It was not until the 41st F4H-1 that the J79-8 was installed, giving increased thrust with after-burning of 17,000 lb (7,711 kg) and a new maximum speed of Mach 2.4. The new engine installation involved an increased angle of 10° for the fixed inboard ramps on the air intakes, and a corresponding increase in the size of the inlets and the angle of the variable ramp. Ramps and the variable stators in the engines were controlled by an AiResearch air-data computer for optimum engine performance over the full speed range of the aircraft.

Carrier trials with the sixth pre-production Phantom began in February 1960 aboard USS *Independence*, subsequently transferring to the considerably smaller flight deck of the *Essex* Class carrier USS *Intrepid*. For carrier-operation the front under-carriage leg was made able to be extended pneumatically to increase the angle of attack at takeoff; power steering was also provided. In October a new order was placed for another 150 production Phantoms: with the adoption of the new unified USN/USAF designation system in September 1962, the basic Phantom designation became F-4, so that the 47 F4H-1s ordered up to the end of 1958

became F-4As, and the definitive production model was designated F-4B. The later F-4As were delivered to squadrons VF-101 and VF-121 for transition training and further trials in December 1960 and February 1961 respectively, followed closely by the first F-4Bs. Full operational service began in October 1961 aboard USS *Saratoga*, and in June 1962 the first Phantom was officially delivered to the US Marine Corps. By 1966 Phantoms equipped 20 US Navy fleet fighter squadrons and nine fighter or fighter-attack squadrons of the USMC.

The Phantom's introduction to service was accompanied by the most spectacular series of record flights ever achieved by a single type. The first record attempt came in December 1959, when the second Phantom built was used in Operation Top Flight. On 6 December Commander Lawrence E. Flint Jr accelerated to a level speed of well over Mach 2 at a height of nearly 50,000 ft (15,240 m) before pulling back into near-vertical

flight and, after the engine flamed out for lack of oxygen, ending with a ballistic trajectory which reached a new absolute altitude record of 98,556 ft (30,040 m).

In September 1960 two closed-circuit records were claimed by F4H-1s, when a triangular course of 500 km (310.7 miles) was covered at an average speed of 1,958.19 km/h (1,216.76 mph) and a 100-km (62.1-mile) circuit was flown at 2,237.41 km/h (1,390.26 mph). The former record was achieved with full afterburner for a continuous period of over 25 minutes, and the latter involved a continuous load in excess of 3 g for the duration of the circuit. Moreover, the distances actually flown had to be greater than the nominal circuit distances to allow for the turns, yet the shorter course was accomplished at just under 5 km (3 miles) greater than the

Phantoms on one of the final assembly lines, before being painted. The 193rd F-4D is nearest to the camera, with the 15th F-4J immediately behind it.

Bottom view of an F-4E in flight over a
range. An auxiliary fuel tank is carried on
each wing and two AIM-9J Sidewinder
missiles on the right. A Pave Spike airborne laser designator is mounted on the
left side of the fuselage and six 500-lb
(227-kg) low-drag bombs on the centreline.
*Inset:* A late model F-4E with the slatted
wings introduced on production Phantoms
from June 1972, following an alarming
number of crashes caused by stalls during
violent manoeuvres at low speeds or
heavy weights.

nominal 100 km, a remarkable achievement at an average speed of Mach 2.24.

Further speed records followed in 1961. Three aircraft flew from Los Angeles to New York in May 1961, alternating full-power dashes with three tanker rendezvous at subsonic speeds. Each broke the record in turn, the third Phantom completing the 2,446-mile (3,936-km) course in the fastest time of 2 hr 47 min for an average speed of 870 mph (1,400 km/h). This high-altitude long-distance achievement was followed in August by a 3-km (1.86-mile) flight at under 100 m (328 ft), appropriately code-named Operation Sageburner. The eighth F4H-1 was used for this attempt, which succeeded in registering an average speed of 1,452.869 km/h (902.769 mph) for four runs over the course, while maintaining a height of around half the maximum allowed.

Three months later Operation Skyburner was aimed at the absolute speed record, which involved flights in opposite directions over a 15/25 km (9.3/15.5-mile) course. Not only had the aircraft to maintain its altitude within 100 m (328 ft) over the course itself, but no diving acceleration was allowed, and altitude throughout the attempt had to be maintained within 500 m (1,640 ft). The aircraft used was the second F4H-1 prototype, flown by Lieutenant-Colonel Robert B. Robinson, USMC, and the attempt was concluded successfully to establish a new record of 2,585.1 km/h (1,606.3 mph), not far short of Mach 2.6. Sustained altitude, involving no deviation greater than 100 m (328 ft) over the 15/25-km course, which had to be flown at a constant speed, was next on the agenda, and this was accomplished at a final height of 20,190 m (66,237.8 ft), an improvement of more than

20% on the previous record.

Finally, having claimed all the available speed and altitude records, Operation High Jump combined the two in a series of flights aimed at the time-to-climb records. These were carried out between February and March 1962, and succeeded in establishing new times for reaching 3,000 m (9,843 ft), 6,000 m (19,685 ft), 9,000 m (29,528 ft), 12,000 m (39,370 ft), 15,000 m (49,213 ft), 20,000 m (65,617 ft), 25,000 m (82,021 ft) and 30,000 m (98,425 ft). The last mark was reached in 6 min 11.43 sec, and was followed by a ballistic zoom which took the

F4H-1 to well above 100,000 ft (30,480 m), though this was not recognised as an official record. Fastest climb was that to 12,000 m, which was reached in 77.15 sec, equivalent to 30,618 ft/min (9,332 m/min).

With the Phantom busy claiming virtually every available performance record, it could hardly escape the notice of the US Air Force that the Navy had come up with a fighter apparently better than anything in its own inventory. In the early 1960s the TFX, ultimately built as the General Dynamics F-111, was being developed to fulfil all the Air Force's future fighter and

tactical aircraft requirements but, in view of the fact that one of the major functions of the TFX programme was to provide the two services with a common aircraft, the USAF was instructed by the Department of Defense to evaluate the Phantom.

Comparative trials during 1961 with the Convair F-106 Delta Dart revealed the F4H-1 to be superior in almost every respect, from needing nearly a third less maintenance in terms of maintenance man hours per flight hour to having a radar interception range nearly 25% greater. Payload/range performance was also better, with the Phantom demonstrating an impressive load-carrying ability. As a result, it was announced in March 1962 that fighter and tactical reconnaissance versions of the Phantom were to become standard equipment with Tactical Air Command, US Air Forces Europe and the Pacific Air Force. Original designations were F-110A and RF-110A, but these were changed later that year to F-4C and RF-4C, with full production being authorised at the end of December.

In their original form, the USAF Phantoms were basically similar to the Navy's F-4Bs, and externally identical, but there were many equipment changes. The new engine designation J79-15 signified no greater change than the incorporation of self-starting equipment, and the folding wings and arrester gear for carrier operation were retained. Dual controls were installed, the provision for these having been part of the original design, although they were not fitted to Navy Phantoms, and the flight refuelling system was changed to use a receptacle on top of the fuselage to match the booms deployed by USAF tanker aircraft. Electronic equipment was also substantially revised, as detailed below.

The USAF received its first F-4Cs in November 1963, and the first RF-4Cs followed in April 1964. The production of Phantoms as standard equipment for Navy, Marine Corps and Air Force represented a remarkable achievement on the part of the McDonnell design team, but this was only the start of a career with both American and other forces that was to establish the Phantom as the pre-eminent combat aircraft of its era.

The assembly line in May 1966, with some of the 825 F-4Ds built for the USAF and Iranian air force alongside Marine Corps RF-4Bs and Air Force RF-4Cs.

*Left:* An F-4B of carrier wing CVW-9, based on USS *Enterprise*, over South Vietnam in April 1966.
*Below:* One of the first pair of F-4Bs transferred to the USAF for evaluation, seen carrying the badge of Tactical Air Command on its tailfin.
*Bottom:* An RF-4C of the 10th Tactical Reconnaissance Wing, USAF Europe, based at RAF Alconbury, photographed in February 1975. The basic F-4C has been superseded in regular USAF service, but during 1983 the McDonnell Douglas plant at Tulsa completed the refurbishing of F-4Cs for the Air National Guard; the tactical reconnaissance version remains in service with both regular and reserve squadrons.

Above: The first of 36 F-4Ds supplied to the Imperial Iranian Air Force in the late 1960s, with its brake parachute deployed.
Left: A Turkish air force F-4E.
Below: An F-4E of the Greek air force.
Right: The first export version of the Phantom, a Royal Navy F-4K, touches down aboard a carrier.

Royal Air Force Phantom FGR.2 (F-4M)
of No. 6 Squadron over its airbase.

Phantoms of No. 892 Squadron, Fleet Air Arm, over a North Sea oil rig in October 1977, shortly before their transfer to the Royal Air Force following the retirement of HMS *Ark Royal. Inset:* The start of a catapult launch from *Ark Royal* in 1973.

*Above:* The first prototype XF4H-1 on an
early test flight showing original air intake
and cockpit canopy shape.

*Below:* Test flight of an F-4E with TISEO
camera on the wing leading edge and
EROS collision-avoidance equipment
under the fuselage.

The 5,000th Phantom, decorated with the
flags of the customer-countries for the
various models, in a vertical climb.

# Phantom Variants

The first designation to be applied to the Phantom under the new system which came into force in September 1962 was **F-4A**. This covered two prototypes originally designated XF4H-1 plus a total of 45 preproduction and initial production F4H-1Fs, the suffix indicating the use of General Electric J79-2 or 2A engines instead of the intended J79-8.

A total of 26 F-4As were used for research and development, the production standard being approximated for the first time with the nineteenth example, and 23 were used by training squadrons from December 1960. Pre-production examples were also evaluated by the USAF, and were used to establish a total of

14 world records for performance, as well as winning the Bendix Trophy for a flight between Ontario Field, some 30 miles east of Los Angeles, and Floyd Bennet Field, New York.

Subsequently, a number of F-4As were modified to **F-4B** production standard; others which continued in use for training purposes were redesignated T-4A. Production was widely sub-contracted, with airframe components supplied by such firms as Aeronca, Beech, Bendix (landing gear), Brunswick, Cessna, Douglas, Fairchild-Republic and Northrop, and assembled by McDonnell Aircraft Company (since 28 April 1967 a division of McDonnell Douglas Corporation) at Lambert Field, St Louis, Missouri. McDonnell itself was responsible for approximately 45% of the structure.

The semi-monocoque fuselage is built in rear, middle and front sections, the last being assembled

in two halves with wiring and equipment installed before joining together. Control surfaces and undercarriage are operated hydraulically, and there is a pneumatic system for the canopy and the nosewheel extension. Electrical power is supplied by an AC generator. Internal fuel capacity of the F-4B was 2,000 US gallons (1,665 Imp gall/ 7,600 litres), and fuselage and wing fuel tanks can also be carried.

Apart from the APQ-72 radar, electronic equipment of the F-4B included a General Electric ASA-32 autopilot, an Eclipse-Pioneer navigation computer and a Raytheon radar altimeter. A Magnavox APR-27 receiver was normally fitted to give warning of missile launches. The standard armament of four Sparrow semi-active radar-guided missiles carried under the fuselage was controlled by the APQ-72; a further two Sparrows or four Sidewinders could be carried

The Phantom was designed to meet a US Navy requirement for a fleet defence fighter, and the first production models were for the Navy and Marine Corps. *Left:* F-4As of VF-101 and VF-121, responsible for fleet training with the Atlantic and Pacific Fleets respectively. *Below left:* F-4Bs of VF-101 in March 1963. *Below:* A pair of F-4Bs of VF-92, operating from USS *Enterprise*, over South Vietnam in 1966.

One of the QF-4B remotely controlled drone conversions produced as supersonic manoeuvring targets for use by the US Navy Missile Centre at Point Mugu, California.

under the wings, the latter being used in conjunction with the infra-red seeker under the nose. In addition, up to 16,000 lb (7,257 kg) of assorted bombs, rockets, guided missiles or other stores could be carried on four wing and one fuselage centre-line stations, and a Lear AJB-3 bombing system was fitted for the surface attack role. Subsequently, pods carrying 20-mm Vulcan cannon were carried both for ground attack and short-range air defence.

A total of 649 F-4Bs had been delivered by the time production ended in March 1967, and these were used initially by 20 US Navy fighter squadrons and nine US Marine Corps fighter or fighter-attack squadrons. Meanwhile, in May 1965 the USMC received its first **RF-4B**, a tactical reconnaissance version produced after the development of the USAF's RF-4C, of which a total of 46 were delivered. No armament was carried by the RF-4B, and a longer nose was used to carry cameras. Equipment was similar to that of the RF-4C, including inertial navigation, side-looking radar and infra-red sensors.

F-4Bs were also converted to

other configurations. These included a total of 12 modified with AN/ASW-21 digital data link communications equipment in place of one of the fuselage fuel tanks and an approach power compensator. Carrying the temporary designation F-4G, these aircraft were used for data link development and for trials with an automatic carrier landing system following the delivery of the first example in March 1963. Some also operated from USS *Kittyhawk* off Vietnam from late 1965, before reverting to standard F-4B form.

A later conversion gave rise to the first **QF-4B** remotely controlled drone towards the end of 1971. This was produced by the Naval Air Development Centre at Warminster, Pennsylvania, and along with subsequent conversions was used for a wide variety of research and trials, often in conjunction with special DF-4B or DF-8L Crusader director aircraft. Primary role of the QF-4B was as a target for missile development, in which role it was required to manoeuvre at supersonic speeds.

More recently, 30 RF-4Bs were scheduled for extensive updating. New equipment to be fitted included AN/ASN-92 inertial navigation system, an automatic carrier-landing system, infra-red linescan equipment by Honeywell and AN/APD-10

side-looking radar. The first RF-4B began conversion to the new standard in 1977. Other conversions of standard F-4Bs have included three modified as YF-4J development aircraft for the improved F-4J production model in the mid-1960s, and another 148 rebuilt as F-4Ns, both of which are described below.

Meanwhile, the 310th Phantom was flown on 27 May 1963 as the first production **F-4C** for the US Air Force, and when production ended in May 1966 a total of 583 had been built. The dead-reckoning navigation system of the F-4B was replaced by a Litton ASN-48 inertial navigation system, improved APQ-100 radar was fitted, and Lear-Siegler AJB-7 all-altitude bombing control equipment was fitted along with guidance equipment for the AGM-12 Bullpup series of radio command-guided missiles. Fuel capacity was reduced slightly. During 1966 a total of 23 squadrons comprising the 8th, 12th, 15th, 33rd, 81st and 366th Tactical Fighter Wings were equipped with F-4Cs. Again, F-4Cs were frequently equipped with podded 20-mm Vulcan cannon for close combat over Vietnam and, for ground attack work, as many as 15 GAU-2A/B pods, each containing a 7.62-mm Minigun with ammunition, could be carried in

*Above:* An RF-4C of the 10th Tactical Reconnaissance Wing, USAF, based at RAF Alconbury in February 1975.
*Right:* One of the F-4Bs transferred to the US Air Force prior to the Phantom's adoption by the latter service, on a test flight from Nellis AFB, Nevada, in 1962.
*Below:* Westinghouse QRC-335A radar jamming pod on the wing pylon of an F-4C.
*Bottom:* An F-4C at Edwards AFB, California, in September 1973. LAU-3A pods for 2.75-in rockets are carried in groups of three on the inboard wing stations, a fuel tank is carried on the fuselage centreline, and two Sparrows are under the forward fuselage.

U.S. AIR FORCE · FJ-

*Above:* The third production F-4C, armed with six BLU-1B napalm bombs at Edwards AFB in June 1964.

*Left:* The elongated nose of an RF-4C, housing cameras for tactical reconnaissance.

clusters of three under the wings and fuselage.

In the early 1970s 36 F-4Cs were supplied to Spain, and after being overhauled by CASA these entered service with two squadrons of the Ejercito del Aire (air force), based at Torrejón, where they were still in service in 1982. At one stage it was planned to exchange these for F-4Es, but in the event further supplies were limited to another four F-4Cs as replacements for examples written off. In Spanish service the Phantom is designated C.12.

Two USAF squadrons in Vietnam were equipped with Wild Weasel versions of the F-4C. The Wild Weasels were specialised defence-suppression aircraft carrying extensive ECM (electronic countermeasures) equipment both internally and in pods. Radar warning receivers for locating missile radars, jamming equipment, chaff dispensers and anti-radiation missiles were standard equipment.

Like the USMC F-4B, the **RF-4C**, first flown in May 1964, had a lengthened nose to accommodate some of the comprehensive collection of sensors with which it was equipped. These included APQ-99 radar for ground-mapping and low-altitude navigation; various cameras for use at high or low altitudes, looking forward or to the sides; infra-red detection equipment to locate camouflaged personnel or equipment; and side-looking aircraft radar to make a high-definition film record of the terrain on either side of the flight path. Camera film could be developed in flight and the cassettes ejected for delivery to ground commanders, and high-frequency radio enabled communications with ground bases to be maintained at all times. No armament was carried, but a variety of ELINT (electronic intelligence) and ECM pods could be carried for locating and jamming hostile

The bigger radome fitted to the F-4D housed a Westinghouse APQ-109 radar, and the new model for the USAF also dispensed with the infra-red seeker.

radars. By the time RF-4C production ended in December 1973, a total of 505 RF-4Cs had been built. Four were supplied to Spain as CR.12s in 1978.

The success of the Phantom in USAF service resulted in a new variant, the **F-4D**, being ordered in March 1964. The infra-red detector was removed, as it was also from a number of F-4Cs, while improved equipment for the air-to-ground role was fitted in place of the forward fuselage fuel tank, following the example of the F-4B/F-4G conversion. A more bulbous nose housed the new APQ-109 radar, which provided air-to-ground ranging, and a General Electric ASQ-91 weapons release computer and AiResearch ASG-22 lead-computing gyro and amplifier for the new servoed optical sighting system went into a new equipment bay vacated by the fuel tank. An improved inertial navigation system was also provided, to give the F-4D a completely automated navigation and weapons delivery system that enabled bombing

accuracy to be improved by up to 200%.

In addition, the new equipment enabled the Phantom's already considerable armoury to be further expanded. Apart from the standard Sparrows and Sidewinders and podded Vulcans for air-to-air use, and the Bullpup introduced with the F-4C, earlier Phantoms were able to carry conventional bombs ranging in size from 250-lb (113-kg) to 1,000-lb (454-kg), nuclear, chemical, napalm and leaflet bombs, rocket launchers and land mines.

With the F-4D, the new TV-guided Walleye glide bomb, whose nose-mounted television camera relays a picture of the target to a monitor in the launch aircraft, allowing course corrections after launch, could be used, as could the TV-guided versions of the Hobos and Maverick introduced subsequently. Walleye was produced in two versions, one carrying an 850-lb (386-kg) warhead over

An F-4D of the 8th Tactical Fighter Squadron armed with Sparrows and laser-homing bombs over North Vietnam, September 1972.

a range of some 16 miles (26 km) and the other with extended range and data link carrying a 2,000-lb (907-kg) warhead and able to be controlled by a second aircraft to give it a range of 35 miles (56 km). Maverick uses a rocket motor to boost its 130-lb (59-kg) warhead to a range of 14 miles (22.5 km). The Hobos system uses a TV or infra-red seeker fitted to standard 2,000-lb (907-kg) Mk 84 or 3,000-lb (1,361-kg) M118E1 bombs.

The addition of ASQ-153 Pave Spike or AVQ-10 Pave Knife laser designators allowed F-4Ds to launch the Paveway series guided bombs, which home on laser energy reflected from the target. Paveway kits can be used with a variety of bombs ranging from the 500-lb (227-kg) Mk 81 to the 3,000-lb M118, or with Pave Storm cluster bombs. Another class of weapon introduced on the F-4D was the radar-homing bomb, used against missile guidance radars, of which the first example was the AGM-78 Shrike.

Another technique developed with the F-4D was known as Pave Phantom, and involved the linking of the weapon release computer with a Loran (long range navigation) receiver. The

intention was to enable Phantoms to bomb with a high degree of accuracy targets which were not visible because of the weather or simply because they were concealed by the jungle. The technique was used as part of the Igloo White programme, in which enormous numbers of seismic and acoustic sensors were deposited along the Ho Chi Minh Trail which formed the main supply lines between North Vietnam and the guerrilla forces fighting in the south. When the sensors were activated by noise or disturbance in their vicinity

*Above:* An early F-4D for the Imperial Iranian Air Force, which bought 36 of this model, carrying a gun pod on the fuselage centreline. *Below:* A USAF F-4D during trials with a modular guided glide bomb over Eglin AFB, Florida, in September 1971. The Phantom was the principal carrier of the various types of guided bomb developed during the Vietnam war.

they relayed a signal, usually via orbiting electronics aircraft, to a surveillance centre in Thailand, where the signals were analysed and air strikes directed against the selected targets. Using Pave Phantom it was possible for the aircraft to be vectored onto the target and release their bombs

*Left:* The first F-4EJ on an early test flight in January 1971. Apart from the first two, F-4EJs for the Japan Air Self-Defence Force were built by Mitsubishi in Japan.
*Below:* Rear view of a USAF F-4E on the dry lake bed at Edwards AFB.

The first of 175 F-4Fs built for the Federal German Luftwaffe. The F-4F is a development of the F-4E optimised for the air superiority role, but with no provision for Sparrows.

An F-4E in markings of the Turkish air force during a test flight from St Louis in July 1974. Turkey bought 40 F-4Es and eight FR-4Es.

automatically on a signal from the computer at the surveillance centre.

Production of the F-4D continued until the end of 1967, by which time a total of 825 had been built. Of these, 32 were for the Imperial Iranian Air Force, the first deliveries being made in September 1966, while 36 ex-USAF F-4Ds were supplied to South Korea from August 1969.

The next variant produced for the USAF, the **F-4E**, introduced a major change in the shape of an internally mounted M-61A1 Vulcan six-barrelled 20-mm cannon, carried under the nose. Structural changes to accommodate this formidable weapon, which has a rate of fire of 6,000 rds/min, plus 640 rounds of ammunition, included the balancing of the extra weight by the inclusion of an extra fuel cell under the tailfin. At the same time, the J79-17 engine, giving increased thrust with after-burning of 17,900 lb (8,119 kg) was installed, and the smaller, lighter, solid-state APQ-120 radar was fitted in a slimmer nose radome, while the slotted tail-plane developed for the US Navy's F-4J was also used.

The first production F-4E was flown in June 1967 and deliveries to the USAF began the following October, an eventual total of 913 being delivered, making it the Air Force's major Phantom variant. During the production run further changes were introduced. Among these was the adoption of leading-edge slats in June 1972: these slats replace the blown flaps fitted to earlier models and are normally retracted flush against the wing leading edge. At high angles of attack, however, they automatically extend to increase lift by as much as one third. The reason for their adoption was the large number of crashes resulting from stalls when heavily loaded aircraft were subject to violent manoeuvres, especially at low

*Top:* One of 88 RF-4Es built for the Federal German Luftwaffe. It combined the basic RF-4C equipment with an F-4E airframe.

*Above:* An AGM-45A-3 Shrike radar-homing missile under the wing of an F-4E at China Lake, California, in November 1973.

airspeeds, during dogfights or when attempting to evade surface-to-air missiles. The improvement offered was so great that almost all earlier F-4Es were modified with the slats, even though this meant rebuilding much of the wing structure.

From early 1973, another innovation was introduced in the form of the Northrop TISEO (target identification system, electro-optical). This consists of a zoom-lens TV camera carried in a cylindrical housing on the port wing leading edge, and allows airborne or ground targets to be identified more readily.

Large numbers of F-4E Phantoms have also been supplied to air forces outside the United States. The first export

customer was Israel, which ordered its first 44 F-4Es in 1968 after the supply of Mirage 5s had been prohibited by France. Deliveries began in September 1969 and continued until late 1976, by which time a total of 204 had been supplied, the majority being ex-USAF aircraft. By 1982 six Israeli fighter squadrons were operating F-4Es. Iran followed up its earlier purchase of F-4Ds with the acquisition of 177 F-4Es, delivered between April 1971 and the middle of 1977. July 1971 saw the delivery of the first two **F-4EJs** to Japan; another 11 were supplied in kit form for assembly by Mitsubishi in Japan, where a further 127 were built. Japanese Phantoms

*Above:* A test flight of one of the 14
RF-4EJs built by McDonnell Douglas for
the Japan Air Self-Defence Force.

*Below:* Six 500-lb (227-kg) Mk 82 bombs
are released from an F-4E of the 347th
Tactical Fighter Wing over Nevada in
1980.

*Top:* One of the 88 RF-4Es supplied to the Federal German Luftwaffe is posed in front of the McDonnell Douglas works in September 1970. *Above:* An F-4E of the 3rd Tactical Fighter Wing, Pacific Air Forces, photographed in January 1981 with a Northrop F-5E Tiger II of one of the USAF's Aggressor squadrons. The latter are painted in Warsaw Pact camouflage schemes and practise WP combat tactics. The 3rd TFW is based at Clark AFB in the Philippines and forms part of the 13th Air Force.

differ in some of the equipment fitted, as do other export machines; by early 1982 these equipped six squadrons of the Japan Air Self-Defence Force's Air Defence Command.

In March 1974 the first of an eventual total of 64 F-4Es was delivered to the Greek air force, three of whose squadrons were using the type in 1982. Turkey

was the next customer, receiving the first of 72 F-4Es in August 1974 and equipping four squadrons. South Korea received 37 F-4Es from October 1975, three squadrons using these alongside the F-4Ds delivered earlier and, in 1979, following the signing of the peace treaty with Israel, Egypt was supplied with 35 F-4Es, though the associated maintenance problems led to Egypt seeking US approval for their sale to Turkey. This was given at the beginning of 1983. Ten F-4Es were supplied to the Federal German Luftwaffe for training in August 1977, and 24 were leased to the Royal Australian Air Force for less than three years from October 1970 while its F-111Cs were being modified.

As with the F-4C, a reconnaissance version of the E model was produced, this time combining basic RF-4C equipment with the F-4E airframe. The **RF-4E** was essentially an export model, and most of the customers for the F-4E also bought small numbers of the reconnaissance model. The Luftwaffe acquired a total of 88, subsequently initiating a programme to modify these for the attack role as well as reconnaissance, and other deliveries, following the production of the first German examples in 1970, include 12 for Israel, 16 for Iran, eight each for Greece and Turkey and 14, with the designation RF-4EJ, for Japan.

The main Luftwaffe Phantom was the **F-4F**, ordered instead of a planned single-seat fighter version designated F-4EF. The F-4F was bought as a straight fighter, with the internal gun, slatted wings, reduced fuel and revised avionics, omitting the air-to-surface delivery systems. A total of 175 F-4Fs were delivered between June 1973 and April 1976, equipping two fighter and two fighter-bomber wings, while two reconnaissance wings use the RF-4E. Subsequently, the F-4Fs were to be updated with a digital navigation and attack system.

The USAF also began a programme to convert some of its F-4Es as Advanced Wild Weasel aircraft for the defence suppression role. A total of 116

A Federal German Luftwaffe F-4F carrying a USAF serial number on a test flight from St Louis prior to delivery.

*Opposite and above:* F-4G Wild Weasels of the 37th Tactical Fighter Wing. Armament of the aircraft opposite comprises Sparrow air-to-air, Standard ARM and AIM-4G Falcon infra-red seeking missiles and a Pave Spike pod.

F-4Es have been converted under this programme, some of which have been modified to eliminate the smoky exhaust from the J79-17 engines. The most significant addition, however, is the APR-38 radar detection and homing system. This equipment improves on the performance of earlier Wild Weasel types by providing the ability to establish the range as well as the bearing of hostile radars, using an array of 52 antennas in various parts of the airframe. The range of frequencies that can be detected has also been expanded to counter the increasing sophistication of surface-to-air missile guidance radars.

The increasing number of mobile SAM systems has also led to improved armament being provided, since a radar, once detected, needs to be dealt with at once rather than by a later air strike, which may not arrive until the launcher and radar system have moved elsewhere. The original AGM-45 Shrike was supplemented by the AGM-78 Standard ARM in 1968, the latter having a range of 15 miles (24 km) compared with the earlier weapon's 10 miles (16 km), and the more recent

AGM-88 Harm (high-speed anti-radiation missile) is designed to give improved performance at comparable ranges. A radar-homing head for the Sidewinder has also been developed.

Many improvements made on later models of the Phantom were incorporated in the **F-4J**, the second production variant for the US Navy, designed to combine optimum interception performance with improved attack capability. For carrier operation, approach power compensation and ASW-25 one-way digital data link provided automatic landing capability, and lift at low speeds was increased by the use of boundary-layer control, bigger flaps, ailerons which drooped automatically to $16\frac{1}{2}°$ when the landing gear was lowered, and slotted tailplanes. Increased weight was catered for by the use of J79-10 engines, rated at 17,900 lb (8,119 kg) with after-burning. The use of Westinghouse APG-59 pulse-Doppler radar gave improved detection capability, particularly of low-flying targets and, along with the AJB-7 bombing system from the F-4C, formed part of a new integrated missile control system designated AWG-10.

The F-4J was flown for the first time in May 1966, squadron deliveries beginning later that year, and 522 were built before production ended in December 1972. At the end of 1982 it was

announced that Britain was to buy 12 ex-US Navy F-4Js to form a new Phantom squadron.

The earlier Phantoms supplied to Britain were also based on the F-4J, but with substantial design changes to incorporate a high proportion of British equipment. The most fundamental change was the replacement of the J79 engines with a pair of Rolls-Royce RB.168-25R Spey 201 engines. These were considerably more powerful than the General Electric powerplant, being rated at 12,500 lb (5,557 kg) dry and 20,515 lb (9,305 kg) with after-burning, but also shorter, fatter and slightly heavier. As a result, the aft fuselage had to be largely redesigned to accommodate them, and the air intakes were made 6 in (15 cm) wider to cater for the increased air flow demanded. All this took time: when the decision to install the new engines was taken in February 1964 it was thought that the standard airframe could be used, but it was June 1966 before the first **F-4K** was flown, and April 1968 before the first three of 52 examples were delivered.

The engines were not the only change to be incorporated in the F-4K. The limitations of British aircraft carriers led to several other alterations, including the redesign of the radar installation. The complete antenna could be swung around along with the

US Marine Corps F-4Js of VMFAT-101 fighter-attack training squadron in vertical flight.

An F-4J of Marine Fighter Attack
Squadron VMFA-531, from USS *Forrestal*,
about to be catapulted from the deck of
HMS *Ark Royal* during joint Royal Navy/
US Navy 6th Fleet exercises in the
Mediterranean.

radome, instead of being pulled
forwards on rails as in the
American versions, enabling
overall length of the aircraft to be
reduced to within the 54 ft
(16.5 m) limit. Lower wind
speeds over British carrier decks
led to the nose wheel leg being
made to extend an extra 20 in
(51 cm), and a stronger arrester
hook being fitted.

Originally, it was planned to
buy a total of 143 Phantoms for
the Royal Navy, but changes in

defence policy, including the
decision to retire the aircraft
carriers *Eagle* and *Ark Royal*, led
to 28 Phantom FG.1s, as the
type was designated in British
service, being supplied directly
to the Royal Air Force, and the
remainder being transferred to
the RAF from November 1978.

Meanwhile, a second British
Phantom variant, designated
**F-4M**, was ordered for the Royal
Air Force in February 1965. This
was intended as a multi-role
fighter, reconnaissance and
ground attack type, being given
the designation FGR.2 in RAF
service, and differed in several
respects from the F-4K. The
folding wings and arrester gear

were retained, but the nosewheel extension and slotted tailplane were not used. The first
example was flown for the first
time in February 1967, and a
total of 118 were delivered
between July 1968 and October
1969.

Equipment fitted to the FGR.2
includes a Ferranti nav/attack
system, both high-frequency and
UHF/VHF communications, IFF
and strike camera. For reconnaissance, an EMI pod can be
carried on the fuselage centreline: this contains a complete
range of sensors, including
cameras, side-looking radar and
infra-red linescan equipment.
Alternatively, an SUU-23 Vulcan

A Royal Navy Phantom FG.1 (F-4K) of
892 Squadron, Fleet Air Arm, is launched
from the deck of HMS *Ark Royal*.

pod can be fitted, in addition to
a wide range of ground-attack
weapons. For airborne interception, the British Phantoms
were armed originally with the
standard Sparrow and Sidewinder missiles. More recently,
these have been supplemented
by British Aerospace Sky Flash
missiles, based on the AIM-7E2
Sparrow but with new seeker and
fuse of British design. Fire control
is the AWG-12, similar to the
AWG-10 and -11 used on the
F-4J and F-4K.

Between 1970 and 1975 the
RAF had four squadrons of
FGR.2s based in Germany, with
another three, plus one with
FG.1s, in the UK for air defence.
Between 1974 and 1977 most of
these converted to Jaguars, while

several new squadrons were
formed, so that by the beginning
of 1982 only two squadrons were
flying FGR.2s with RAF
Germany, while three had
FGR.2s and two FG.1s at three
bases in Britain. Two Royal Navy
squadrons were formed with
FG.1s in 1969, but one of these
was disbanded in 1972, and the
other served aboard *Ark Royal*
until 1978.

Remaining Phantom desig-
nations are applied to earlier
models subject to modernisation,
re-equipment and partial
rebuilding. The **F-4N** conversion
was applied to a total of 178
F-4Bs by the Naval Air Rework
Facility at NAS North Island,
California, with the first conversion being completed in
February 1973. The airframe was
strengthened to further prolong
their service life, which had
already lasted considerably longer

than had been envisaged in the
original design. At the same time
more modern avionics, similar to
those used on the F-4J, were
installed, including the one-way
data link.

Tests of another conversion,
the **F-4S**, during 1977 were
followed by the updating of 265
F-4Js to the new standard. The
first stage of this programme
involved structural strengthening
and the installation of the digital
AWG-10A weapon control
system to improve air combat
capability, particularly at close
ranges. The first stage of this
conversion was carried out by
the Naval Air Rework Facility,
and the modernised aircraft were
then scheduled to undergo further
work at the McDonnell factory.

This second stage involved the
installation of modified J79-10B
engines, and the fitting of the
leading-edge slats as used on the

*Above:* RAF Phantom FGR.2s (F-4Ms) in flight over the Forth bridge. British models, with Rolls-Royce Spey turbofans, are the heaviest, most powerful and slowest of all Phantoms.

*Below:* To accommodate the fatter Spey engines, the aft fuselage of British Phantoms had to be extensively redesigned, as shown in this photograph of an RAF FGR.2.

US Navy F-N conversions of F-4Bs in flight. A total of 178 F-4Bs were converted with strengthened airframes and updated avionics.

The experimental F-4CCV control-configured Phantom was fitted with canard foreplanes to improve turn and altitude performance.

later F-4Es and subsequent models. The main role envisaged for the F-4S was to equip the Marine Corps air combat squadrons until Phantoms were replaced by the new F/A-18 Hornet.

There have been various experimental conversions of Phantoms, as well as others, such as the F-4VG variable geometry version proposed for the US Navy and RAF as substitutes for the F-111B and Anglo-French Variable-Geometry strike-fighter respectively, which were never built. (Nor, it might be added, were the F-111B and AFVG.)

One experimental version which did valuable work was an RF-4C fitted with full-authority quadruple fly-by-wire as the Survivable Flight Control System. The F-4SFCS was first flown in April 1972, and formed the basis for the fly-by-wire system used in the General Dynamics F-16 Fighting Falcon currently in production for half a dozen air forces. Subsequently, the SFCS was rebuilt as the F-4CCV, retaining the fly-by-wire system but incorporating Control-Configured Vehicle technology. Among the new features of the F-4CCV were canard foreplanes

positioned above the front of the engine inlets, whose purpose was to generate vortices over the upper surfaces of the wings to prevent boundary-layer air breaking away and thus increasing lift and improving control. At the same time, the outboard sections of the trailing-edge flaps were modified to act as flaperons giving direct-lift control. In addition, a slab of lead under the tail moved the centre of gravity aft, thus reducing stability. With these modifications the F-4CCV proved to be able to fly higher and turn more quickly than standard F-4s, but there was never any prospect of the fantastic sums of money being available to introduce these modifications as standard.

When Phantom production by McDonnell came to an end in 1979 some 5,100 F-4s had been turned out by the St Louis factory in nearly 20 years of continuous production. The first 1,000 were completed on 7 July 1965, with the handing over of a Marine Corps RF-4B, a Navy F-4B and an Air Force F-4C. An F-4D became number 2,000 on 21 February 1967, and over the next 18 months the production rate approached two Phantoms

a day, a US Navy F-4J being delivered as the 3,000th example on 28 August 1968. During the 1970s production gradually slowed, with the USAF receiving the 4,000th Phantom, an F-4E, on 1 February 1971 and the Turkish air force taking delivery of number 5,000, another F-4E, on 24 May 1978. The last Phantom of all was an F-4EJ, the 138th built by Mitsubishi, which was handed over to the Japan Air Self-Defence Force on 20 May 1981.

The only Western combat aircraft to have exceeded the Phantom in numbers built are the North American F-86 Sabre and the Bell UH-1 Huey helicopter. Neither of these involved the expenditure of comparable sums of money, an estimated twenty billion dollars having been spent on Phantoms and their associated spares. In the early 1980s the biggest single customer for the type, the US Air Force, still had an estimated 1,700 in service, while another 600 continued to serve the US Navy and Marine Corps.

Phantom number 5057, the last to be built at St Louis, in USAF markings before being handed over to the Republic of Korea.

# Phantoms in Service

The war in Vietnam, immoral and ultimately unwinnable though it was widely held to be, was as severe a test of aircraft and the men who flew them as has been devised. On the other hand there was the sheer physical difficulty: operating with no front line to speak of, the strike aircraft were called on to deliver close support to ground troops they couldn't even see, or fly long-range missions over the north, over hostile and unforgiving terrain, where the weather was usually dreadful and the chances of getting home after baling out remote. On the other there were the political constraints: the long-range interdiction missions that were the Phantom's staple diet were concentrated on military targets in the Haiphong and Hanoi areas, which meant bridges for the most part, while the crews were under strict orders to avoid civil targets, neutral

shipping in Haiphong harbour, or built-up areas of any kind.

The opposition was different from that encountered in any previous war, too. There were plenty of MiG-21s, flying ground-controlled interceptions under the command of a sophisticated radar network, and the rules of engagement demanded a positive visual confirmation before an attack could be launched. This meant that American pilots frequently had to close to a range less than that over which the Sparrows that formed their primary armament were effective.

In the long-range interception role for which the Phantom was originally designed, the Sparrow was intended to be launched at a range of from 12 to eight miles (19–13 km), following detection at up to 40 miles (64 km) and missile lock-on at about 15 miles (24 km). The heat-seeking Side-

winders were designed to be launched at closer ranges, but the Phantom pilots were often obliged to get too close even for a Sidewinder for the prescribed visual confirmation, and it was to overcome this disadvantage that the internal gun was introduced on later models, starting in 1967 with the F-4E.

However, enemy fighters did not constitute the only, or even the major threat. Vast numbers of anti-aircraft guns, ranging from quadruple 12.7-mm (0.5-in) and twin 14.5-mm (0.57-in) weapons to single guns of 37-mm (1.46-in), 57-mm (2.24-in), 85-mm (3.35-in) and 100-mm (3.94-in) were deployed, the bigger weapons with radar control, giving effective coverage at all altitudes up to 20,000 ft (6,100 m). And above that height radar-guided surface-to-air missiles came into their own.

Consequently, new tactics had

GBU-15 guided glide bomb under the wing of a TISEO-equipped Pave Strike F-4E.

Pre-takeoff routine for an F-4 on the deck
of USS *Midway* in August 1970.

ALQ-119 ECM pod, one of a wide range of electronic warfare devices which Phantoms have carried, under the forward fuselage of an F-4.

to be devised to overcome the various threats, and with the introduction of the versatile F-4 in the theatre in 1965 these began to be elaborated. Ultimately, they involved a high degree of specialisation in a variety of different areas, ranging from new methods of aerial combat — designed to be effective with unprecedented approach speeds of well over 1,000 mph (1,600 km/h) becoming normal — to refined techniques of electronic warfare, with the entirely new mission of defence suppression becoming standard practice.

In the face of the combination of AAA (anti-aircraft artillery) and SAMs (surface-to-air-missiles), the pilots were faced with two basic options on the approach to a target. Either they could fly high, keeping out of range of the guns but leaving themselves open to missile attack, or they could fly low, hoping to evade the radar surveillance. Having chosen the former course, the appearance of a SAM hurtling towards them at Mach 3 necessitated an immediate dive for the ground, out

of the way of the SAM but, as often as not, straight into an artillery barrage.

The first phase of sustained air operations against North Vietnam went under the code name Rolling Thunder and lasted from March to December, 1965. An early target was the Thanh Hoa bridge, carrying road and rail traffic over the Song Ma river some 70 miles (113 km) south of Hanoi. This bridge was to become something of an obsession with the military planners, and it was during the first raid mounted, on 3 April 1965, that the first opposition from MiG-17s was encountered.

It was soon realised that the tactics employed by the defending fighters involved waiting until the strike aircraft were on their way home, and consequently low on fuel, before making hit-and-run attacks, vectored by ground controllers, on the last flight of the formation. The first successes against the MiGs were gained on 10 July 1965 by four F-4Cs, exploiting this knowledge and following behind the main formation: the need for visual identification prevented the use of Sparrows, but after a series of high-g supersonic manoeuvres that took one of the Phantoms

Navy and Marine Corps F-4s among the equipment on the deck of USS *Midway* in 1974.

from 20,000 ft (7,000 m) down to 12,000 ft (3,660 m) and up again to 33,000 ft (10,000 m), two attacking MiG-17s were destroyed by Sidewinders.

Three weeks later the first F-4C was downed by a SAM, and it was soon realised that an immediate response was required in the form of violent evasive manoeuvres and jettisoning all stores. Unfortunately, it was in this context that the stall-spin characteristic began to be a major problem. Violent manoeuvres with the Phantom heavily loaded, or at low air-speeds, tended to produce a stall, followed by a usually fatal spin from anywhere under 10,000 ft (3,000 m). It was revealed at a Congressional inquiry in 1971 that 79 Navy, and an unspecified – but much greater – number of Air Force F-4s, had been lost in this way, and it was as a direct result that the slatted wings were introduced on the F-4E.

The effect of the combined opposition, when Rolling Thunder resumed in February 1966, was to severely degrade the accuracy of the bombing attacks, with the strike aircraft having to dodge their way into the target area and drop their ordnance first time, while the F-4s flying MiG-CAP (combat air patrol) rarely encountered fighter opposition. The intro-duction of Wild Weasel F-105F Thunderchiefs carrying ECM pods to jam the missile radars enabled the strike aircraft to return to flying at an altitude of 5,000–6,000 ft (1,500–1,800 m), out of the range of the worst of the AAA and with a degree of immunity to the SAMs, but then the Wild Weasels began to be attacked by the faster MiG-21s.

Consequently, the North Vietnamese fighter defences became a prime target, and one method tried early in 1967 under the code name Operation Bolo met with some success. This was an expansion of the earlier use of F-4Cs to simulate F-105s, but now the equivalent of an entire strike force of Phantoms was employed. No fewer than 14 flights of four F-4Cs, along with four flights of F-104 Starfighters and six Iron Hand flights of F-105s with ECM and radar-homing missiles, carried out a sweep over Phuc Yen airfield, to the north of Hanoi. In the resulting engagements, seven MiGs were shot down by F-4Cs.

Such methods could only succeed when they came as a surprise, and the tactics of the air war were constantly revised, with an ever-increasing use of electronic support. In May 1967 attacks began on North Vietnamese airfields, with the object of destroying the fighters on the ground, and the introduction later in the year of EC-121M Warning Stars enabled the MiGs to be detected as they left the ground, giving the American pilots valuable advance notice. But then the introduction of optical tracking equipment for the missiles began to nullify the effect of the Wild Weasels. Between April 1968 and the following October, when all bombing operations over North Vietnam were halted, bombing was restricted to the southern part of the country, where there were no SAMs and no ground control for the interceptors.

While the raids on the north were suspended, many USAF Phantoms were switched to the specialised task of seeding the Ho Chi Minh trail with acoustic and seismic sensors used to detect the movement of trucks on the main route south through Laos. This operation, known as Igloo White, was designed to interrupt the flow of trucks on which the Viet Cong guerrillas fighting in the south depended, and developed into a massive

programme of surveillance and interdiction.

Phantoms were used to deliver the sensors, which were produced in a variety of exotic forms and transmitted a signal when they detected noise or movement in their vicinity. To provide useful information they had to be positioned with great accuracy, which was made possible by the inertial navigation systems fitted to the USAF F-4Cs and F-4Ds. The signals broadcast by the sensors were picked up by orbiting relay aircraft and analysed at the Infiltration Surveillance Centre in Thailand, where banks of computers stored and sorted the information and selected the most promising targets for air strikes, which again were commonly delivered by F-4s. It was in these operations that the inertial navigation systems of the Phantoms were employed in conjunction with Loran radio navigation in the Pave Phantom system.

Using the navigation systems in combination with the weapons delivery computer, the Phantoms were able to launch strikes against unseen targets. The information derived from the Igloo White sensors having been used to compute the position for the strike, this was programmed into the aircraft computer, which automatically vectored the fighter into position and released the ordnance over the desired location.

Another technique used in the interdiction programme involved the pairing of an F-4 with an AC-47 gunship. The AC-47s, and later models of gunships, carried several miniguns with massive quantities of ammunition, and were equipped with infra-red and other sensors to enable them to locate movements on the ground. They were thus able to direct the Phantoms, carrying various types of munitions, marking targets detected by their sensors with flares or illuminating them with

An early bombing sortie by a US Navy F-4B from USS *Midway* over South Vietnam in November 1965.

laser designators so that laser-guided bombs could be launched.

Close air support was another common task for F-4s, carried out both by land-based USAF aircraft and Navy Phantoms operating from carriers stationed in the Gulf of Tonkin. In this respect, again, it was accurate target information that was the main requirement. Bombing on map coordinates supplied by ground commanders proved insufficiently precise, and forward air controllers in light aircraft orbiting over the combat area came to be the standard method of directing support strikes. The FACs could provide constant instructions to the fighter-bomber pilots, giving visual aiming cues to correct their aim as they rolled in at high speeds to avoid the hail of small-arms fire.

The last major deployment of Phantoms to Southeast Asia came in April 1972, following the full-scale invasion mounted that month by the North Vietnamese army. In an impressive series of operations, Phantom squadrons from bases in North Carolina, Florida and New Mexico flew their aircraft across the Pacific, refuelling several times en route from accompanying KC-135 tankers and making intermediate landings in Hawaii and at Guam. Within a week of receiving orders to move, these units were in action from bases in Thailand, providing further evidence of the reliability of the F-4. A total of

108 F-4Ds and 72 F-4Es were assembled at bases in Thailand in a matter of days, while Navy squadrons aboard carriers began operations from the Gulf of Tonkin.

The invasion of the south was followed by the resumption of bombing attacks on North Vietnam in a new series of operations under the code name Linebacker. By this stage the air defences were more concentrated than ever before, and to reach their targets the strike groups had to be carefully coordinated to provide defences against the various threats. The F-4s now formed the bulk of the strike force, with a variety of specialised roles being carried out within each formation.

Typically, a Linebacker strike force would be preceded by two flights of F-4s or A-7 Corsairs sowing 'chaff', bundles of radar-reflective material of the type first used during the Second World War. To be effective, the chaff had to be released at precise heights and carefully timed to form a screen behind which the main force could follow. Consequently, the chaff aircraft were required to fly in precise formations, straight and level and at reduced speeds, using ECM pods to jam the missile radars and escorted by MiG-CAP flights of F-4Es. Further defence suppression would normally be provided by Iron Hand flights, consisting of two Wild Weasel F-105s to seek out the radar sites and with radar-homing missiles to launch against them, accompanied by a pair of F-4Es carrying Sparrow missiles for air defence and cluster bombs to drop on the AAA emplacements.

The strike group itself might comprise up to eight flights of F-4Es carrying conventional and laser-guided bombs, escorted by anything up to 18 more F-4Es configured for the air combat role. Further F-4Es would be deployed to provide top cover against fighter attack and, last of all, some way behind the main force, would come a pair of RF-4C reconnaissance Phantoms to record the aftermath of the raid and enable the damage caused to be assessed. Thus a force of 32 strike aircraft might be supported by 46 other aircraft in the ECM, chaff-sowing, defence-suppression, escort and reconnaissance roles, and further support would be provided by electronics aircraft providing long-range stand-off jamming and radar surveillance to warn of fighters taking off, and tankers for in-flight refuelling. All of this required the strike aircraft to fly in a precise formation, which was facilitated by the use of the same basic aircraft to perform most of the various tasks.

Of course, the whole point of these operations was to destroy specific targets, and in this respect technological advances had provided the means for much more accurate bombing attacks. The major contribution was made by the development of new types of smart bomb, whose effectiveness was most clearly demonstrated by the history of the attacks on the Thanh Hoa bridge.

As outlined above, the first raids against the Thanh Hoa bridge were carried out during operation Rolling Thunder in 1965, by F-105 Thunderchiefs using conventional bombs and Bullpup missiles. The Bullpups were standard 250-lb (113-kg) or 1,000-lb (454-kg) bombs fitted with a rocket motor, steerable fins and radio links so that they could be steered by an operator in the launch aircraft. However, this procedure involved the launch aircraft maintaining visual contact with missiles all the way to the target, imposing a severe strain on the crews in heavily defended areas.

In June 1965 carrier-based strike aircraft of the US Navy took over the responsibility for attacking the Thanh Hoa bridge, carrying out 24 raids in the ensuing 12 months. Despite the fact that the railway south of the bridge had been cut in several places, and that pontoon bridges were being used to bypass it while damage was repaired, the destruction of the bridge itself continued to be a major objective, and attacks continued whenever the weather permitted until the bombing halt at the end of March 1968.

A USAF F-4C fires its rockets over Vietnam in March 1966.

When the bombing was resumed in April 1972 new weapons were available in the form of the Hobos and Paveway series of guided bombs which eliminated the need for continuous active guidance by the crew, allowing them to take evasive action immediately after launch. Hobos uses a television camera mounted on the nose of a standard 2,000-lb (907-kg) or 3,000-lb (1,361-kg) bomb to relay a picture to the operator in the launch aircraft, enabling him to designate the target before launch and leave the bomb to home on the indicated objective. The Paveway bombs use a laser-seeking head, again in conjunction with standard bombs, to home on laser energy reflected from the target: the laser designators carried by Phantoms could be locked onto the target and would continue to track it despite the manoeuvres of the aircraft.

Phantoms were the main vehicles for these new smart bombs, having both the navigation systems to enable them to find the targets and the accommodation for a Weapon Systems Operator to carry out the pre-launch target tracking. The first strike against the Thanh Hoa bridge was carried out on 27 April, with four Phantoms laying down a chaff corridor for another eight armed with smart bombs. The weather being unsuitable for the use of laser designation, five 2,000-lb Hobos bombs were launched, and succeeded in causing extensive damage to the structure, though without actually demolishing it.

A second strike on 13 May took advantage of clearer weather to launch nine 3,000-lb and 15 2,000-lb laser-guided weapons against the bridge, along with a total of 48 conventional 500-lb weapons — a total of 81,000 lb (36,740 kg) nominal weight, and a considerably higher actual weight — carried by 14 F-4s. This time one of the steel spans of the bridge was knocked completely off its pier.

This was not the last attack against the Thanh Hoa nor was the Thanh Hoa the only bridge to be subject to repeated attacks. It proved the most difficult to destroy, however, and provides the most dramatic illustration of the effectiveness of the new types of weapon deployed on the Phantom. At the same time, it is one of the minor tragedies of the whole sorry war that so much effort should have been expended on destroying what was actually an almost irrelevant target. Subsequent analysis has estimated the cost of the attacks on the Thanh Hoa bridge, including the loss of some 50 strike aircraft, at over a billion dollars and, while the defenders were forced to

An F-4 of the Israeli air force with a selection of the varied ordnance it can carry.

devote considerable resources to defending and repairing the structure, the interruption of supplies caused, which was the ostensible reason for its destruction, was almost negligible.

While the Phantom was being developed from its original role as a fleet defence interceptor to become one of the most versatile and hard-working of all combat aircraft, its potential in the air combat role was also steadily improved. The most obviously useful addition was that of the built-in gun on the F-4E, but equally important were the improvements in the electronic systems, and in the defensive systems carried. The latter have included the whole range of modern electronics, from radar-warning receivers and jammers to chaff and flare dispensers and even miniature aircraft, designed to produce an identical radar signature, which can be released from underwing pods. Offensive avionics also improved, and as more modern radar systems were installed it became possible to confirm the identity of hostile aircraft without waiting until they were in visual range. An even more useful device, though it was not fitted to F-4Es until early 1973, was the TISEO system, using a television camera on the wing to identify targets at the long ranges made possible by a zoom lens.

The necessity for modern combat aircraft to be equipped with effective ECM was clearly demonstrated in the other theatre where Phantoms have seen extensive combat, namely the Middle East. In 1967, in a carefully coordinated pre-emptive strike, the Israeli air forces were able to destroy the bulk of the Egyptian air force on the ground, and in the ensuing brief but hard-fought war the Israeli Phantoms were able to concentrate on providing effective support for the ground forces.

In 1973, however, the

Phantoms of the Israeli air force found themselves up against the same threat that the Americans had faced in Vietnam, in the form of Soviet guided surface-to-air missiles. The result was such heavy losses that for a time the Phantoms had to be withdrawn from the close support role until the missile sites were overrun. As a result, just as the American success in Vietnam had tended to undervalue the missile threat, the setbacks suffered by the Israelis led some analysts to conclude that air support for ground troops was no longer a viable form of operation when the opposition included guided missiles.

However, as always in the history of warfare, a successful weapon soon inspires effective countermeasures. Thus, during the fighting in the Lebanon in 1982, the Israelis proved able to eradicate the missile threat, confusing the batteries with electronic warfare and deception techniques so as to be able to destroy them with conventional bombs in low-level attacks. Naturally, the precise techniques used have not been revealed, but the fact remains that a missile is only as good as its guidance system, and if the guidance can be disrupted then the missile ceases to be effective.

The current specialists in anti-missile work with the United States Air Force are the pilots and Electronic Warfare Officers of the 562nd Tactical Fighter Training Squadron, part of the 37th Tactical Fighter Wing which operates the majority of the F-4G Advanced Wild Weasel Phantoms in service. A total of 116 F-4Gs were produced by converting F-4Es, a few of which are believed to have been lost, and other Advanced Wild Weasel squadrons are based in the Philippines and in Germany. The importance of the EWO in Wild Weasel operations is such that he is accorded equal status with the pilot, and the standards

demanded of the crews mean that to be officially considered experienced they need to have logged at least 100 hours in an F-4G, with at least another 400 hours in tactical fighters and a minimum 1,000 hours total flying.

The basis of the F-4G's defence suppression capability is the APR-38 detection and homing system, whose 52 antennas deployed along the length of the airframe allow radar signals to be detected at several points so that the range can be calculated by triangulation. The armament carried is not restricted to the obvious choice of radar-homing missiles — one easy way to negate the effects of these is to close down the SAM radar and broadcast an identical signal from a dummy transmitter, which will suspend the threat temporarily but does not provide a long-term answer. Consequently, the missiles are likely to be used alongside more conventional weapons such as a cluster bomb, which cannot be decoyed by a fake transmitter and will prove at least as effective as a Shrike if it can be deposited in the middle of the battery.

So the Phantom continues to play a full part in the front line of the USAF strike forces, applying the lessons of old wars to the requirements of the future. In carrying out missions that were not even thought of when it was designed, it continues to show the versatility and adaptability that have been the hallmarks of its career.

# The Future

In the early 1980s, F-4s of various marks were in service with the air forces of ten different countries, as well as continuing to serve with all three air arms in the United States. Of an original total of 2,885 delivered to the US Air Force, nearly two thirds were still in service, while others had been transferred to the Air National Guard and a total of at least 225 had been passed to other air forces. Combined deliveries to the US Navy and Marine Corps amounted to 1,270, with rather less than half still serving in 1981.

Among the USAF units equipped with Phantoms during 1981, Tactical Air Command numbered 22 in the United States, including ten with F-4Es, four with F-4Ds, five with RF-4Cs and the three squadrons of F-4Gs with the 37th Tactical Fighter Wing at George AFB, California. Apart from the last, these squadrons form four Tactical Fighter and two Tactical Reconnaissance Wings. Another squadron each of F-4Es and a mixture of reconnaissance, electronic and E models respectively were based at the Tactical Fighter Weapons Centre at Nellis AFB, Nebraska, and at Eglin AFB, Florida, with the Tactical Air Warfare Centre, while a single Fighter Interception Squadron was stationed in Iceland.

The number of Phantoms

The elegantly painted F-4CCV, featuring fly-by-wire and direct-lift control, in flight.

based in Europe had been reduced, but there were still 11 Phantom squadrons with USAF Europe at the time, including a reconnaissance squadron in England, three F-4D fighter squadrons based alongside the Spanish air force Phantoms at Torrejón, and the remainder stationed in Germany. These comprised five fighter squadrons of F-4Es, a reconnaissance squadron of RF-4Cs and an Advanced Wild Weasel squadron with F-4Gs.

The Pacific Air Forces had very few Phantom units left by this stage, though there was still a squadron each of F-4Es and RF-4Cs based in South Korea and Japan, and another of F-4Es based alongside the F-4G unit in the Philippines. Remaining regular Air Force units were operated by Communications Command, which had the last squadron of F-4Cs and another three of F-4Ds.

Air National Guard service by 1981 was extensive, with 23 of the ANG's total of 90 squadrons using various models of Phantoms. Specific units included five Fighter Interception and the same number of Tactical Fighter Squadrons with F-4Cs, four TFS and one FIS with F-4Ds, and eight Tactical Reconnaissance squadrons with RF-4Cs.

The original F-4B had disappeared from US Navy service, but a number of units remained active with later rebuilds and a few F-4Js. With the Naval Air Force Atlantic Fleet there were two squadrons of F-4S and one

of F-4Js serving with Fighter Wing 1, based at Oceana, Virginia. The Pacific Fleet's Fighter and Airborne Early Warning Wing, divided between California and Japan, included two squadrons of F-4Ns and three of F-4S. Carrier groups deployed aboard the aircraft carriers *Coral Sea* and *Midway* during 1981 each included two squadrons of Phantoms.

The Marine Corps by 1981 had relegated its remaining Phantoms to reserve wings, Reserve Carrier Air Wing 20 at Dallas and RCAW 30 at Miramar, California having two squadrons each of, respectively, F-4N and F-4S. Other examples were operated by various US Navy test establishments.

The Phantom is no longer the fastest aircraft in the world, nor the highest-flying, and its old time-to-climb records have been rendered obsolete by manned spacecraft — though it is worth noting that in the early days of the American space programme the Phantom was given the job of following the space vehicles from the launching pad to record the early phases of the flights on film. Nevertheless, it is significant that the new holders of those records are specialised high-performance types, the MiG-25 and the Lockheed SR-71, whose other capabilities are severely limited in comparison with the all-round versatility of the F-4.

At the same time, there are newer fighters that can get off the ground quicker, climb faster and carry out interceptions at longer ranges, but it was fifteen years after the Phantom was in service before they appeared, and it will be surprising if any of them is produced in comparable numbers. Meanwhile, the Phantom is a long way from retirement. New systems, exemplified by those of the F-4G, will continue to adapt it to meet new requirements and to fill new roles.

# Specifications

## F-4B

| | |
|---|---|
| **Type:** | all-weather multi-role fighter |
| **Accommodation:** | 2 |
| **Armament:** | six AIM-7 Sparrow or four Sparrow and four AIM-9 Sidewinder air-to-air missiles; 16,000 lb (7,257 kg) external stores |
| **Powerplant:** | two General Electric J79-GE-8 turbojets, 10,900 lb (4,944 kg) st dry, 17,000 lb (7,711 kg) st with reheat |

**Performance:**

| | |
|---|---|
| maximum speed | 1,485 mph (2,390 km/h) at 48,000 ft (14,630 m) |
| cruising speed | 575 mph (925 km/h) |
| initial climb rate | 28,000 ft/min (8,534 m/min) |
| service ceiling | 62,000 ft (18,900 m) |
| range | 400 miles (645 km) |

**Weights:**

| | |
|---|---|
| empty equipped | 28,000 lb (12,701 kg) |
| normal take-off | 44,600 lb (20,230 kg) |
| maximum take-off | 54,600 lb (24,766 kg) |

**Dimensions:**

| | |
|---|---|
| span | 38 ft $4\frac{7}{8}$ in (11.71 m) |
| length | 58 ft $3\frac{3}{4}$ in (17.77 m) |
| height | 16 ft 3 in (4.95 m) |
| wing area | 530 sq ft (49.242 sq m) |

## F-4D

| | |
|---|---|
| **Type:** | all-weather multi-role fighter |
| **Accommodation:** | 2 |
| **Armament:** | six Sparrow or four Sparrow and four Sidewinder; 16,000 lb (7,257 kg) external stores |
| **Powerplant:** | two J79-GE-15 |

**Performance:**

| | |
|---|---|
| maximum speed | 1,485 mph (2,390 km/h) at 48,000 ft (14,630 m) |
| cruising speed | 578 mph (930 km/h) |
| initial climb rate | 28,000 ft/min (8,534 m/min) |
| service ceiling | 70,000 ft (21,337 m) |
| range | 900 miles (1,450 km) |

**Weights:**

| | |
|---|---|
| empty equipped | 28,000 lb (12,701 kg) |
| normal take-off | 46,000 lb (20,865 kg) |
| maximum take-off | 54,600 lb (24,766 kg) |

**Dimensions:**

| | |
|---|---|
| span | 38 ft $4\frac{7}{8}$ in (11.71 m) |
| length | 58 ft $3\frac{3}{4}$ in (17.77 m) |
| height | 16 ft 3 in (4.95 m) |
| wing area | 530 sq ft (49.242 sq m) |

## F-4EJ

| | |
|---|---|
| **Type:** | all-weather multi-role fighter |
| **Accommodation:** | 2 |
| **Armament:** | one M61A-1 20-mm gun; six Sparrow or four Sparrow and two Mitsubishi AAM-2 or Sidewinder; 16,000 lb (7,257 kg) external stores |
| **Powerplant:** | two J79-GE-17 |

**Performance:**

| | |
|---|---|
| maximum speed | 1,450 mph (2,334 km/h) at 36,000 ft (10,973 m) |
| cruising speed | 585 mph (941 km/h) |
| initial climb rate | 28,000 ft/min (8,534 m/min) |
| service ceiling | 62,250 ft (18,975 m) |
| range | 600 miles (966 km) |

**Weights:**

| | |
|---|---|
| empty equipped | 30,073 lb (13,641 kg) |
| normal take-off | — |
| maximum take-off | 57,400 lb (26,036 kg) |

**Dimensions:**

| | |
|---|---|
| span | 38 ft $4\frac{7}{8}$ in (11.71 m) |
| length | 63 ft (19.20 m) |
| height | 16 ft 6 in (5.03 m) |
| wing area | 530 sq ft (49.242 sq m) |

## RF-4C

| | |
|---|---|
| **Type:** | tactical reconnaissance aircraft |
| **Accommodation:** | 2 |
| **Armament:** | six Sparrow or four Sparrow and four Sidewinder; 16,000 lb (7,257 kg) external stores |
| **Powerplant:** | two General Electric J79-GE-15 turbojets, 10,900 lb (4,944 kg) st dry, 17,000 lb (7,711 kg) st with reheat |

**Performance:**

| | |
|---|---|
| maximum speed | 1,459 mph (2,348 km/h) at 40,000 ft (12,190 m) |
| cruising speed | 587 mph (945 km/h) |
| initial climb rate | 48,300 ft/min (14,722 m/min) |
| service ceiling | 59,400 ft (18,105 m) |
| range | 840 miles (1,350 km) |

**Weights:**

| | |
|---|---|
| empty equipped | 28,276 lb (12,826 kg) |
| normal take-off | 39,788 lb (18,048 kg) |
| maximum take-off | 58,000 lb (26,308 kg) |

**Dimensions:**

| | |
|---|---|
| span | 38 ft $4\frac{7}{8}$ in (11.71 m) |
| length | 62 ft $10\frac{7}{8}$ in (19.17 m) |
| height | 16 ft 6 in (5.03 m) |
| wing area | 530 sq ft (49.242 sq m) |

## F-4E

| | |
|---|---|
| **Type:** | all weather multi-role fighter |
| **Accommodation:** | 2 |
| **Armament:** | one M61A-1 20-mm gun; six Sparrow or four Sparrow and four Sidewinder; 16,000 lb (7,257 kg) external stores |
| **Powerplant:** | two General Electric J79-GE-17 turbojets, 11,810 lb (5,357 kg) st dry, 17,900 lb (8,119 kg) st with reheat |

**Performance:**

| | |
|---|---|
| maximum speed | 1,485 mph (2,390 km/h) at 40,000 ft (12,190 m) |
| cruising speed | 585 mph (941 km/h) |
| initial climb rate | — |
| service ceiling | 62,250 ft (18,975 m) |
| range | 595 miles (960 km) |

**Weights:**

| | |
|---|---|
| empty equipped | 29,535 lb (13,397 kg) |
| normal take-off | 40,562 lb (18,399 kg) |
| maximum take-off | 61,651 lb (27,965 kg) |

**Dimensions:**

| | |
|---|---|
| span | 38 ft $4\frac{7}{8}$ in (11.71 m) |
| length | 57 ft 7 in (17.55 m) |
| height | 16 ft 6 in (5.03 m) |
| wing area | 530 sq ft (49.242 sq m) |

## F-4F

| | |
|---|---|
| **Type:** | all-weather multi-role fighter |
| **Accommodation:** | 2 |
| **Armament:** | one M61A-1 20-mm gun; four Sidewinder; 16,000 lb (7,257 kg) external stores |
| **Powerplant:** | two J79-GE-17A(MTU) |

**Performance:**

| | |
|---|---|
| maximum speed | 1,485 mph (2,390 km/h) at 40,000 ft (12,190 m) |
| cruising speed | 585 mph (941 km/h) |
| initial climb rate | 28,000 ft/min (8,534 m/min) |
| service ceiling | 56,300 ft (17,160 m) |
| range | 780 miles (1,255 km) |

**Weights:**

| | |
|---|---|
| empty equipped | 30,633 lb (13,895 kg) |
| normal take-off | — |
| maximum take-off | 60,186 lb (27,300 kg) |

**Dimensions:**

| | |
|---|---|
| span | 38 ft $4\frac{7}{8}$ in (11.71 m) |
| length | 63 ft (19.20 m) |
| height | 16 ft $5\frac{1}{4}$ in (5.01 m) |
| wing area | 530 sq ft (49.242 sq m) |

## F-4K (RAF FG.1)

| | |
|---|---|
| **Type:** | all-weather multi-role fighter |
| **Accommodation:** | 2 |
| **Armament:** | four Sparrow or BAe Skyflash and four Sidewinder; 16,000 lb (7,257 kg) external stores |
| **Powerplant:** | two Rolls-Royce Spey 201 turbofans, 12,250 lb (5,557 kg) st dry, 20,515 lb (9,305 kg) st with reheat |
| **Performance:** | |
| maximum speed | 1,386 mph (2,230 km/h) |
| cruising speed | — |
| initial climb rate | 32,000 ft/min (9,754 m/min) |
| service ceiling | 70,000 ft (21,337 m) |
| range: | 500 miles (805 km) |
| **Weights:** | |
| empty equipped | 30,000 lb (13,608 kg) |
| normal take-off | — |
| maximum take-off | 56,000 lb (25,401 kg) |
| **Dimensions:** | |
| span | 38 ft 4$\frac{7}{8}$ in (11.71 m) |
| length | 57 ft 7 in (17.55 m) |
| height | 16 ft 1 in (4.90 m) |
| wing area | 530 sq ft (49.242 sq m) |

## F-4M (RAF FGR.2)

| | |
|---|---|
| **Type:** | all-weather multi-role fighter |
| **Accommodation:** | 2 |
| **Armament:** | four Sparrow or Skyflash and four Sidewinder; 16,000 lb (7,257 kg) external stores |
| **Powerplant:** | two Rolls-Royce Spey 202 turbofans, 12,250 lb (5,557 kg) st dry, 20,515 lb (9,305 kg) st with reheat |
| **Performance:** | |
| maximum speed | 1,386 mph (2,231 km/h) at 40,000 ft (12,190 m) |
| cruising speed | — |
| initial climb rate | 32,000 ft/min (9,754 m/min) |
| service ceiling | 60,000 ft (18,289 m) |
| range | 1,000 miles (1,610 km) |
| **Weights:** | |
| empty equipped | 31,000 lb (14,061 kg) |
| normal take-off | — |
| maximum take-off | 58,000 lb (26,308 kg) |
| **Dimensions:** | |
| span | 38 ft 4$\frac{7}{8}$ in (11.71 m) |
| length | 57 ft 11 in (17.65 m) |
| height | 16 ft 3 in (4.95 m) |
| wing area | 530 sq ft (49.242 sq m) |

## Phantom deliveries

| Model | Quantity | Recipient |
|---|---|---|
| F-4A | 47 | US Navy |
| F-4B | 649 | US Navy and Marine Corps (227 converted to F-4N) |
| RF-4B | 46 | US Marine Corps |
| F-4C | 583 | US Air Force (40 transferred to Spain) |
| RF-4C | 505 | US Air Force (4 transferred to Spain) |
| F-4D | 793 | US Air Force (36 transferred to Republic of Korea) |
| | 32 | Iran |
| F-4E | 949 | US Air Force (116 converted to F-4G Wild Weasel) (150 transferred to Israel) (36 transferred to Egypt, subsequently to Turkey) |
| | 177 | Iran |
| | 86 | Israel |
| | 72 | Turkey |
| | 56 | Greece |
| | 37 | Republic of Korea |
| | 10 | German Federal Republic |
| RF-4E | 88 | German Federal Republic |
| | 16 | Iran |
| | 12 | Israel |
| | 8 | Greece |
| | 8 | Turkey |
| F-4EJ | 140 | Japan |
| RF-4EJ | 14 | Japan |
| F-4F | 175 | German Federal Republic |
| F-4J | 522 | US Navy and Marine Corps (265 converted to F-4S) |
| F-4K | 52 | United Kingdom |
| F-4M | 118 | United Kingdom |

# Acknowledgments

We would particularly like to thank Karen Stubberfield of the McDonnell Douglas Corporation in the UK for her invaluable help with the pictures for this publication.

Picture research was through Military Archive and Research Services, Braceborough, Lincolnshire, and unless otherwise indicated below all material was supplied by McDonnell Douglas.
Crown Copyright (MOD-RAF): pp. 20–21, 43 (top), 43 (bottom).
Crown Copyright (MOD-RN): pp. 19, 22, 41, 42.
Flight International: pp. 6–7.
Israeli Air Force: p. 52.
MARS: p. 28 (inset).
US Air Force: pp. 17, 28–29, 30 (bottom), 31 (bottom).
US Navy: pp. 34 (bottom), 39, 44 (top), 47, 48–49, 50.